MW01173147

Cute Animal
Coloring Book

**Let your imagination soar by using
the colors of your choice**
This adult coloring book has Over Different & Creative
Designs, with richly detailed line art, originally created
by our favorite artist to give you the best coloring
experience. Each page is unique, with a different breed
as well as a different sort of theme, as each dog is doing
something else and often staged with various items.

THE END